WEST YORKSHIRE · W.Y.Q.S · QUEER STORIES

Editors: E-J Scott, Ross Horsley and Ray Larman.
Designed by Zed - They Them Studio

This publication was made possible with funding
from National Lottery Heritage Fund and the
Garfield Weston Foundation.

The project was produced in partnership with
Yorkshire Mesmac, West Yorkshire Archive Service
and Leeds Museums & Galleries.

Film still from *My Butch (A Yorkshire Stubbornness)*,
produced by West Yorkshire Queer Stories' Sound Artist,
Debbie Sharp (they/them), in the 1990s.

# CONTENTS

# amen etc.

Well, we're into our third issue, the summer weeks seem to fly past and the GEMINI in Huddersfield is still open and very busy.

But enough of that boring gossip. Anyway those wayward owners have allowed us to print a photo so at least you know who they are if they run off with your money.

PETE & STEVE (gemini)

On the subject of music (and what better one) it just amazes me how some of you lads tolerate some of the dirge and dog thrown at you in the name of entertainment. Where do you DJ's pick up some of your records. I believe one establishment doesn't even know that Patrick Cowley is dead and to record your latest sounds of Radios 1,3 and 2 (in that order) is just breaking the law. So come on bring yourselves up to date, splash out on a few of those highly poplar American 12's. Forget the Beatles and the Nolans, buy yourself some new gear (or get your boss to) and move with the times. You cant blame the equipment all the time. If HERO'S, GEMINI, Alans NEW PENNY, Le PHONOGRAPHIQUE, FLAMINGO and JUNCTION can do it, so can the rest.

AMEN - but not quite. To all you lads visiting Blackpool, I am assured that RUMOURS is the new in pub. So avoid it unless you wear white jeans, yellow jeans or any other colour but blue 'cos the jerks on the door obviously don't know what jeans are!!

# BOYSTOWN © REVIEW

FREE

June July Issue No. 3

Huddersfield — Bradford
Leeds — Blackpool and London

© Boystown Promotions Ltd. 1983.

**BOYSTOWN REVIEW** was a bi-monthly gay culture guide with an emphasis on the north of England, produced by the Boystown Group (Boystown Promotions Ltd) in Glossop, Derbyshire. It was available free from venues in Huddersfield, Bradford, Leeds, Blackpool and London in the early 1980s.

Contributed by Gerry Millar

Between June 2018 and March 2020, West Yorkshire Queer Stories gathered oral histories from a diverse range of LGBTIQ+ [lesbian, gay, bisexual, trans, intersex and queer] people across the region, as part of an archiving initiative supported by the National Lottery Heritage Fund and Yorkshire MESMAC. The resulting recordings, together with a collection of objects, have since taken their place in local museums and archives, helping to diversify their collections and change the way we think about the people's history of West Yorkshire.

The integrity of the West Yorkshire Queer Stories project lies not only within the breadth of voices represented in its collection of stories, but also within the collecting process itself. After a successful pilot project conceived by Jude Woods, WYQS secured funding to recruit new project workers and train over 70 volunteers– our Community Curators– to carry out interviews. This training empowered these volunteers to record stories responsibly and securely. In turn, this allowed participants to speak freely, enabling them to share their stories straight from the heart, uninhibited. By listening to each other, members of the community also learned more about each other, strengthening community ties across the region.

Participants were signed up by our Community Curators who visited groups, took over social media, and spread the word widely throughout queer communities. Venues across West Yorkshire, including Leeds City Museum, the National Science and Media Museum, Bradford and the Hyde Park Picture House, helped create exciting free events to encourage participation. The length of the individual interviews ranges from full life-stories to snapshots of a particular era, and also includes group interviews, written memoirs, and videos.

This publication showcases newly commissioned photography, poetry and film stills, as well as keepsakes of queer culture and a selection of story highlights. The collection is simply too big to publish in its entirety, despite every single contribution being unique, important and revealing, in equal measure. All of the full-length interviews are housed at the West Yorkshire Archives and a combination of both short clips and full stories are featured on our website (wyqs.co.uk), with increased accessibility supported by transcripts and BSL interpretation.

The success of the entire project rests on the incredible knowledge, enthusiasm and commitment of our amazing volunteers and participants, to whom this book is dedicated. They came out, spoke up and secured their rightful place in history.

# THE WEST YORKSHIRE QUEER STORIES TEAM

### Ray Larman Community Development Worker

It's been an absolute pleasure to meet so many amazing LGBTIQ+ people from around West Yorkshire who have been so generous in sharing their stories. I've learnt so much about local queer history from working on this project and I really hope that people explore the WYQS collection to get a sense of all the different voices and histories that make up our LGBTIQ+ communities.

### Ross Horsley Community Development Worker

This project has opened my eyes to the depth and diversity of LGBTIQ+ communities, as well as the unique history West Yorkshire holds. I hope that the stories we've captured will continue to inform researchers and inspire artists for many years to come, and remind everyone who hears them to take time to listen to others.

### E-J Scott Project Coordinator

With their focus on 'queer' experience, queer oral histories are sometimes critiqued as being yet another force that contributes to 'othering' LGBTIQ+ people. But I've found listening to the enchanting accounts of full queer lives lived in the valleys, towns and cities of West Yorkshire– some radical, some ordinary– nothing short of refreshing. To then have these stories so richly translated into art, creating a legacy of the collection itself, is further proof to me of their inherent value.

### Jesson-Hill WYQS Artists

Jesson-Hill are multimedia artists commissioned by WYQS to create an art film celebrating West Yorkshire's LGBTIQ community. Using surrealism, *Riding West on a Walrus Tail* is a queer fairytale bringing a fantastical perspective on real life stories. Our band of actors and muses shared stories of wit, honesty and bravery that will leave a lasting imprint on the County's queer history.

**Ian Humphreys** WYQS Poet

I was commissioned to write a poetic response to stories by queer people of colour from the WYQS archive. It was a genuine privilege to listen to so many varied and poignant stories, most involving individuals overcoming prejudice and fear, many sharing tales of perilous journeys, and each and every one honouring difference and celebrating the human spirit.

**Matt Mead** WYQS Artist Filmmaker

Undoubtedly, the best thing about this project was the wonderful people I got to work with. The film participants generously offered not only their time, but also their stories, sharing incredibly personal and deeply moving moments from their lives. I was truly privileged to work with such a wonderful community, exemplars of joy, inspiration, resilience, determination, queerness and diversity.

**Debbie Sharp** WYQS Sound Artist

It's important for queer people to tell their stories and for our lives to be reflected in arts and culture. It was great to be able to share part of my own story and to perform *My Butch (A Yorkshire Stubbornness)*. I also loved working creatively with the oral histories; hearing about Queer West Yorkshire through another people's perspective was inspiring.

**Geoff Brokate** WYQS Photographer

I loved collaborating and being involved in this project, because it shows how owning your story and having your voice heard is an empowering exercise. I am in awe of how honest and open everyone was and it showed me how important it is to listen to people; simply listening and allowing people to be vulnerable. This is important, because real social change can only begin once we accept and celebrate each other's differences.

# INTRODUCTION

It's astonishing to think that after two years of traversing West Yorkshire to collect stories from 232 contributors— being welcomed into people's homes, exhibiting in museums, meeting in community pubs, hubs and cafés, taking photos in parks and filming in industrial and rural landscapes— that this publication should have been edited in isolation because of a global pandemic. It has intentionally been produced in response to this health crisis, as a way of using the region's collective queer history to physically bring us together— it's something to touch, hold onto and treasure. It will be posted out for free, reaching into queer households, schools and libraries across West Yorkshire, the rest of the UK and around the world.

This book is packed full of stories about gestures of community kindness, accounts of brave acts of defiance, discos, dancing, singing and romancing. From feminist fundraisers to homosexual helplines, marches to moustaches, the stories are, of course, familiar and echo a national dialogue, yet remain simultaneously unique. Nowhere but West Yorkshire has Jackie, the minibus driving dyke who took women home from the University of Leeds in the late 80s. Not only did she offer them safe travel in the wake of the 'Yorkshire Ripper'

murders (an attempt to help reverse the falling number of women enrolling as a consequence), she also leant them an ear when they came out to her. Only Hebden Bridge could answer all the needs of a trans dad, pregnant with his third child, and his husband, who left Israel in search of a "queer" village to call home. Only the DJs at Huddersfield's Gemini club can say that they famously saw out the 1981 police raid to *God Save the Queen*.

From the outset, Ray and Ross and I were committed to building a collection that prioritised stories from people with disabilities and black, brown and trans people. We strategized, planned and prioritised for this to occur. Fieldwork determined it, underpinned by the efforts of older, radical feminist activists who have always been, and remain, the beating heart of this region's queer values and visibility. One remarkable find includes the conference programme from the UK's first national trans ("T.V./T.S.") conference TRANSVESTISM AND TRANSSEXUALISM IN MODERN SOCIETY that was held on the 15-17th March, 1974, organised by members of the Leeds University T.V./T.S. Group and the Beaumont Society. As well as discussion groups surrounding work, family and social life, plus academic presentations by medical specialists and social workers (followed by a session where the audience could "comment or challenge our Delegates"), the three day affair included a swanky reception at the Guilford Hotel on the Friday, a disco dance on the Saturday, a bookstall and fashion suppliers.

Despite achieving our aims for inclusivity and fair representation of the spectrum of the region's queer demographics in our collecting, predictably, the photographs in this book are mostly of white people. That's because they were the contributors who overwhelmingly had the confidence, and coincidentally, the time to be there when the photos were being taken. On the positive side, when I did a search of transcripts using the keywords "black", "brown", "Asian", "QTIPOC", and unavoidably, "refugee" and "asylum", I added up a total of 'roughly' 2,231 minutes of audio. That's a bit more than 37 hours, which is significant. The addition of personal artefacts from photographic artist, archive curator and radical sex activist Ajamu X– including the ticket stub to the Soft Cell concert he went to at Caesars in 1983, as well as a rare copy of his magazine Blac (there were only ever 500 printed) that he produced in Huddersfield in 1985–

add significant depth to the QTIPOC collection.

With hundreds of people involved in the project, queer community ties have continued to be strengthened across the region. This work builds upon the many decades of community and outreach work in the area that has directly contributed to the saving of queer lives. Our project's lead partner, Yorkshire Mesmac, has historically been at the national forefront of the strategic development and delivery of sexual health outreach and education and has been there from the outset of designing and delivering these services. Put simply, West Yorkshire's queers have never been too afraid to hand out condoms in clubs, defying media scaremongering and myth making. Tom's story has put that on the record. Queers have a history of taking the 's' out of 'scare' and turning it into care. It's what brings all the letters in our alphabet identity soup together. Just as lesbians and trans guys nursed gay men and trans women with AIDS in the 80s, so too, this book brings together a rainbow of queer experiences as a timely reminder of our resounding collective endurance in times of crisis.

History has a terrifying tendency to

repeat itself. Mirroring how the AIDS crisis disproportionately affected gay men, so too, COVID-19 is affecting the LGBTIQ+ community in ways that remain largely unreported outside queer social media. The impact of being isolated in an unsupportive family home is a threat to our young people's mental health. Our QTIPOC friends and those on lower incomes have been more heavily affected. Trans surgeries— already with horrendous waiting times that breach NHS guidelines— have been postponed 'indefinitely', as they have been deemed 'non-essential' by our government's Minister for Women and Equalities during the pandemic. It's a frightening prediction of what may lie ahead for LGBTIQ+ health service funding when we tumble into an inevitable economic recession post COVID-19. Higher rates of HIV and cancer in the broader LGBTIQ+ population, coupled with the fact that LGBT people are 50% more likely to smoke (due, in part, to our enviable sociability and club-centric culture), increases the risk of respiratory infections in our community. How hard have we all been hit by the virus? We'll probably never know, because stigma and discrimination within the medical system means LGBTIQ+ people are still less likely to seek medical help.

I don't mean to be all doom and gloom. In fact, the point of this collection is that we have a long history of proving we are stronger than ever, when we walk together… The queer community's track record of resilience is as remarkable as its legacy of resistance. You only have to listen to Tash on her podcast episode, to know what I'm talking about. Tash describes trapesing through snow up a hill in Hebden Bridge to meet Char, a lesbian from another generation. Despite never having met before, Char welcomes her into her home. In front of a roaring fire, overlooking the valley, microphone on, Char goes on to share her story of working under the introduction of Clause 28 in 1988, in Keighley's Equal Opportunities Unit. You can practically feel the warmth of those mugs of tea, cupped in the hands of lesbian herstory, both past and present.

The warmth of Char's story provides a chilling counterpoint to the current surge of populist politics that endorses, promotes and regulates hetero-gender normativity. More than ever, our collective awareness, vigilance and resistance needs to be ongoing to safeguard the hard-won recognition of LGBTIQ+ equal rights. To this end, the project invited queer curator, art historian, academic and activist,

Tomasz Kitlinski, to visit Leeds, where he outlined the charges laid against him in Poland that could potentially see him imprisoned for two years for speaking out against the introduction of LGBT "No Go" zones in Lublin. Similarly, the COVID-19 virus has distracted our national attention from, but not delayed, a hard Brexit and the UK is about to self-isolate from the European Convention on Human Rights. We must stay vigilant and continue to be brave enough to speak up and speak out in defence of freedom and equality.

Listening to each other's stories is the very best way to understand the spiritual value that's embedded in community togetherness. From Wetherby to Wakefield, Cleckheaton to Castleford, I am deeply grateful to every single person who, like Char, shared their story, and to those of you, like Tash, who helped collect them. You didn't only record queer history, you collectively contributed an important and enduring chapter.

E-J Scott, West Yorkshire Queer Stories Project Co-ordinator.

OVERLEAF

**TRANSVESTISM AND TRANSSEXUALISM IN MODERN SOCIETY**, the UK's first national conference on trans issues, was held at the University of Leeds over the weekend of 16-17 March, 1974. Organised by the Beaumont Society, it was unique in that it was coordinated by trans people, for trans people.

APPENDIX 'D'     Conference Programme (as sent to Delegates)

THE FIRST NATIONAL T.V./T.S. CONFERENCE

AT LEEDS

On 15th, 16th and 17th March, 1974

"TRANSVESTISM AND TRANSSEXUALISM IN MODERN SOCIETY".

Organised by the Leeds University T.V./T.S. Group.

Principal Speakers

Dr. Elizabeth Ferris, MB., BS.,
    (Gender Identity Research)

Miss M. E. Williams,
    (Public Relations Officer,
    Beaumont Society.)

Mrs. C. F. Cordell,
    (Social Worker, Founder of ACCESS)

Miss Julia Tonner,
    (Transsexual Action Organisation
    U.K. Branch.)

Admission to the Conference is FREE, but any Donations towards the costs will be gratefully accepted.

Leeds T.V./T.S. Group,
153 Woodhouse Lane,
Leeds 2.          Tel 39071  Extn. 57

=========

PROGRAMME

All times shown are approximate and may be subject to alteration.

Friday 15th March  7.30 - 10.30pm at the Guildford Hotel, Leeds. Reception and Coffee Evening for Delegates and Friends. Licensed Bar available.

Saturday 16th March  At Leeds University Union Debating Chamber.

10.15 a.m. Opening address: J. B. Willmott (Conference Secretary)
10.30 a.m. Miss Margaret Williams (P.R.O. Beaumont Society)
    "The Psychology of Transvestism and Transsexualism"
11.15 a.m. Miss Julia Tonner (T.A.O., UK Representative)
    "Fit or Misfit?" The position of the Transsexual at work and leisure in modern society.
12.00 - 1.00 p.m. Lunch (Available at the University Refectory)
1.00 p.m. Mrs. C. F. Cordell (Social Worker, Founder of ACCESS)
    "Know Thyself"
1.45 p.m. Dr. E. Ferris (Gender Identity Research)
    "Transvestism and Transsexualism: Their Origins and the Problems of coping with these conditions".
2.30 p.m. Feature Film: "The Queen"
    Behind the scenes at an American 'Drag Contest' featuring Transvestite and Transsexual viewpoints.
4.00 p.m.  Conference Workshops
to    The Conference will divide up into a number of Discussion Groups, each of which will be asked to examine some aspect of Transvestism and Transsexualism and its impact on Family and Social life. The results
5.00 p.m.  will be presented at the Sunday morning Conference Session.
           -: Tea Break :-
7.30 p.m.  Social Evening and Disco Dance for Delegates and Conference Visitors, at
to    the Lipman Building (adjoining Leeds University Medical School)
    Admission (on production of Conference Programme) 25p.
12.00mdnt. Lounge and Bar (Extension to 11.30 pm) Dancing to Top Discs.

===========
34

Sunday 17th March   At Leeds Polytechnic Common Room

11.00 a.m.  Workshops Reports and Discussion of Findings.
12.30 p.m. - 1.30 p.m. Lunch Interval
 1.30 p.m.  Open Forum - A Question and Answer Session, YOUR opportunity to comment
            or challenge our Delegates.
 3.30 p.m.  Closing Address
            Miss June Willmott (Beaumont Society - North of England Regional
                                                        Representative)

================

BOOKSTALL

A wide range of T.V. and T.S. Books and Leaflets available for sale, or to order.

PHOTOGRAPHY: The Official Conference Photographer, Miss Deleyze Anne, of T.V.
Photographics, 130 Osmaston Road, Derby, will be in attendance throughout the
Conference, and will be pleased to take individual, or group pictures on request.

FASHION SERVICES: The following shops and suppliers will be pleased to assist
transvestites and transsexuals in choosing and obtaining all their fashion and
footwear requirements.

Cover Girl Shoes Ltd., 95 Upper Islington, London, N1 ON4
David de Lacy, Theatrical Costumier, 38 Somerfield Road, London N4 (Tel.01-226-8980)
The Nottingham Exclusive Dress Agency, 15 King Street, Nottingham.
The Elite Dress Agency, 1 - 3 Smithy Lane, off King Street West, Manchester 1.
The Tall Girls Shop, 397 Washway Road, Sale, Cheshire.(Tel.061-973-5109)

============

## YOUR  CONFERENCE  GUIDE

(Also see sketch map enclosed)

Friday Evening Reception The Guildford Hotel is at 119 The Headrow, Leeds - just
200 yards East of the Town Hall.

Saturday - Conference Sessions At Leeds University Union Debating Chamber;  The
Union Building is well signposted from all parts of the Campus.

Saturday - Evening Social and Disco Dance At the Lipman Building which is located
adjacent to the Leeds University Medical School, opposite Leeds Dental Hospital
in Blundell Street ($\frac{1}{4}$ mile south of the main University Campus)

Sunday - Conference Sessions Polytechnic Common Room. This is situated in the
main building of the Leeds Polytechnic, Woodhouse Lane, 500 yards south of the
University.

'Bus Services   Leeds City Transport Services.

1 & 4 from Railway Station and City Square. 33, 36 & 56 from Central Bus Station.

Car Parks   Short Term - Outside the Union Building
            Long Term - Public Multi-Storey Car Park in Woodhouse Lane -
                        ($\frac{1}{4}$ mile south of University)

============

A detailed Report of the Conference Proceedings will be published as soon as
possible after the close of the Conference. If you would like a copy please place
your reservation at the Bookstall. The Report will be in booklet form and will
cost 15p.

=== : ===

**BEN, Leeds**

Project volunteer Ben is pictured on Upper
Basinghall Street in Leeds City Centre.

Geoff Brokate Photography

I've come out twice in my life – the first time when I was around 14 as gay, then at 19 as trans. Luckily my family and friends were (and continue to be) very supportive, but I'd never really gotten involved in the LGBTIQ+ community outside of the internet (I grew up in a very small village). I identify as Trans/Non-Binary, I use he/him pronouns and I am demisexual. I am also a massive history geek and I am disabled and neurodivergent. I spent four years in London for my BA at university and I was suddenly surrounded by queer people. Amazing, loving, extravagant, quiet, gorgeous, polite and kind people who were so much more than just 'queer'. They became my family away from home and taught me so much, not just about myself, but also the community I come from.

So when I moved away from London to Leeds for my MA last summer, I found myself without that support around me. Of course, I had the internet, but it's not the same. That's when I found West Yorkshire Queer Stories. As a young historian, I couldn't pass up the opportunity to be part of a queer oral history project. My partner saw an advert they posted saying they wanted more volunteers and suggested I sign up. So I thought 'screw it', throw anxiety to the wind and just dive in. There's no better way to meet such a cross-section of local queer society.

I've met so many incredible people through my time with WYQS. I've been able to help create zines with Non-Binary Leeds, help run stalls at events such as Happy Valley Pride in Hebden Bridge, create interview summaries and interview people myself. Through listening to people's stories, I've felt so much more connected to the queer community around me. Be this through conducting interviews or making up summary sheets, I've interacted with so many more people than I'd dreamed of, and not just people like me, but people I probably wouldn't have met in normal circumstances. People with life experiences wildly different to mine, but just as important. I've learnt so much about local queer history and experiences.

One of my favourite things about the interviews is being able to hear the emotion which comes with each of these stories, and how every single one is unique. I've 'met' (either through interviews and summaries) an Israeli trans-man who has given birth to his children; a lesbian refugee from Uganda; a non-binary Jewish, disabled, activist (hi Leo, you're fab); a gay man from Bangladesh who had to escape for fear of death; and a Yorkshireman who hid his homosexuality when working in the mines, but then went on to create the Yorkshire Bears.

I'd never have left my safe bubble if I hadn't signed up to help this project. This had been the most fun few months. And I'm so proud of all the hard work everyone has put into making this happen. And I am proud of me.

> **I've met so many incredible people through my time with WYQS.**

### EPIE, Leeds

Epie is an asylum seeker who arrived in the UK in 2014 after fleeing Cameroon because of his sexuality. He came to Leeds (where he is pictured in Harehills) in 2018.

Geoff Brokate Photography

Being in Leeds, it's ... like starting all afresh. Being in Leeds was the only place I really felt like I'm at home. I really felt free, like I could really do anything I wanted to do, or what I love doing ... I know only till I got to Leeds that I had all that...all that support.

This badge was designed by Intentional Promotions in the 1980s to simultaneously oppose racism and draw attention to the rights of the lesbian and gay community.

This poem explores a recurring theme in the West Yorkshire Queer Stories collection of QTIPOC (queer, trans and intersex people of colour) having to leave their homes or birthplace to gain acceptance. For author Ian Humphreys, it holds personal resonance. He explains: "At one end of the scale are people, like myself, who leave a rural English village to 'come out' in a big city. At the other end, a gay couple who has to flee Pakistan because of death threats from their families and the Taliban."

## A thousand crossings

Before leaving, they seeded coded words
under sunflowers, milk thistle and jasmine,
submerged in a paddy field,
buried in dust
below a nailed-mute floorboard.

Sacred words,
slipped from one tongue to another.

And for one moment, perhaps just a breath,
fear fled their body until
they swallowed it afresh,
a gutful of granite and ocean.

They moved invisibly,
folded between pages of the Quran, the Bible,
a locked diary. Tucked unseen
inside an amber-beaded purse,
under the chassis of a truck.

When they finally reached their new home
people looked right through them.

At first, they gasped at their own reflection,
startled by doppelgangers
in rainbow-flagged bars and nightclubs.
Most times, the mirror beamed back,
*welcome-sister-brother-auntie-lover.*
Other times, it fractured into dark shards.

It took a lifetime to embrace a new language,
to learn how to shout their own name.

Years after leaving, they dared dream
of words they had planted,
of new voices
stirring apple orchards, palm groves,
sweetening acres of yam,
pushing through clay, concrete and bone,
lifting city smog
and rising like music, song,
early morning prayer.

Ian Humphreys

The women-only disco, Mrs. Big's Benefit Bop, took place on Saturday 30th July, 1988, at the Pavilion on Woodhouse Moor, Leeds.

The Tod Women's Disco is a real institution... It feels like a little bit of history that's kind of just stayed the same. It's monthly; it's at the Cricket Club, which is ... not a particularly kind of gay-friendly space, but I think ... it's one of the really nice things about this valley is the women's disco happens there and it always has happened there, and everyone just accepts that ... I've been– on and off– for about 18 years.

**DAWN, Todmorden**

Dawn met her partner while studying at the University of Leeds. They moved to Hebden Bridge together in 2001.

**JAMES, Leeds**

James, who moved to Leeds from North Yorkshire, went dry stone walling with his dad in this story in 2002.

Geoff Brokate Photography

My Dad gave me silent treatment for about a week... He builds dry stone walls... For some reason, a week after my Mum had told him, he took me out dry stone walling with him, which I don't think I'd done before with him. And I thought, ah, he's just going to kill me in the woods somewhere and just leave me somewhere and [laughs] no one'll ever see me again. But what happened was ... I'd started helping him with the walling and we just started talking about anything other than me being gay. I don't think we touched on it at all, but we just started talking, and everything seemed to be OK after that.

### SUZY, Leeds

Suzy Mason founded club night 'Vague' with her friend, Paul Fryer, at The Warehouse in Leeds (pictured) in 1993. It ran successfully for three years and was followed by the long-running 'Speed Queen', that Suzy created with Kas Shaw.

Geoff Brokate Photography

In the very beginning at Vague, I remember talking to a big promoter in Manchester and telling him what I was gonna do and I said, "I'm gonna open this club in Leeds and it's gonna be mixed and basically I'm gonna put gay people and straight people, and black people and white people, and young people and old people together". And he just laughed at me and he said, "You're crazy, it won't work". You know, he was promoting The Haçienda, he was massive, and he just said, "It'll never work in Leeds, Suzy. There'll be bloodshed". And I thought, "Well, I'm from Leeds and I want this and I'm an ordinary girl, so I reckon loads of other people do".

A ticket to the Victor Victoria
Valentine's Ball, 1998.

Contributed by Ian Baxter

And I remember someone saying to me, "It's not very political, is it, putting on tea-dances and balls?" And I remember standing on the stage in Leeds Town Hall in some outrageous ridiculous outfit in front of a few hundred lesbians and gay men and thinking, "This is fairly political!" Steve, who was part of the team and was really enthusiastic about going dancing in other places, he suggested we should go to Pudsey Civic Hall, where they had, I think, a weekly ballroom dancing session so we went to that [laughs] and it was terrifying, because there were, there were lots of straight people doing their ballroom dancing and then we turn up and there were things called sequence dances where two of you are together and one of you moves on. So there were the terrified faces of the ballroom dancers of Pudsey as they were having to dance with the same-sex partner. That felt pretty political as well.

## IAN, Leeds

Ian and his friends began running LGBT+ tea dances in Saltaire in the late 1990s. Due to their popularity, in 1997 they moved to Leeds Town Hall, where one event was filmed by Channel 4.

## JAMIE, Leeds

Jamie is a theatre director, filmmaker and musician based in Leeds, whose work has appeared at venues across the north of England, including the Leeds Playhouse and Palace Theatre, Manchester.

Geoff Brokate Photography

We all have lots we can learn from the way that trans and non-binary people are talking about gender. Like, maybe you're a cis-gender man who's always been kind of pressured about the femininity that you display, or you're a butch woman and being challenged on the masculinity... All of these tight regimes and shackles that we've placed around our gender– these rigid rules– they're limiting and we need to loosen off those shackles and shake them off, 'cos we're all so much freer when we loosen up those rules. The LGBTQ+ rights movement and liberation is positive for everybody. People need to start to realise that.

**EMILY, Leeds**

Emily runs Leeds Bi Group
that was founded in 2014.

Geoff Brokate Photography

[Leeds Bi Group] marched in Leeds Pride for the first time a few years ago and then we took a break, and then we came back last year. And the difference in the response that we got was amazing. It wasn't that we weren't welcome the first time, but last year when we marched, just everybody was so happy to see a bisexual group marching with the bi [and] pan flags going and the banner with 'Leeds Bisexuals' on it and just so many people that were obviously doing the "Oh my God… That's my flag! That's my colours there!" It was really lovely to see. It was amazing. And then last year was so much better again. It was … such an amazing feeling.

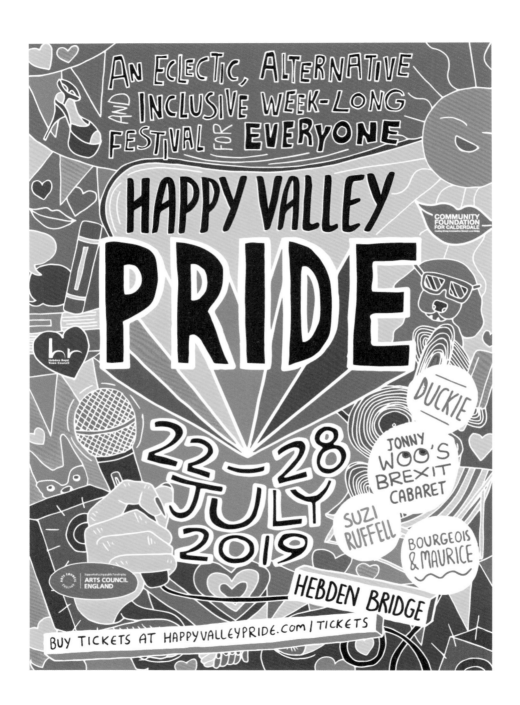

Flyer art by Emma Charleston for Hebden Bridge's Happy Valley Pride, 2019.

I'm married to a guy, and at the time [2017] we had two kids (now we have three). And I knew we were probably also planning a third pregnancy – I was the one who was pregnant. So we needed somewhere quite queer and accepting and open-minded. And actually, most people we know that have left Israel and moved abroad had moved to big cities, and we thought, on the one hand, that would be the easiest choice, because there's kind of big immigrant communities, Israeli communities, if we were interested in them, which we weren't really at the time and we're totally not now. And of course, queer communities. But then, at the same time, we were also dreaming of somewhere with a bit more countryside and rural and – yeah. But [we] were afraid that that sort of … smaller places might be more conservative and we'd be less comfortable there. And then we said, 'There must be somewhere.' So we Googled 'queer-friendly village UK' [laughs] and landed in Hebden Bridge! [Laughs.]

## YUVAL, Hebden Bridge

As a non-binary trans person with a male partner and several children, Yuval and their family had to think carefully about where they could all live safely and without harassment.

Members of the
Huddersfield Socialist
Workers' Party take
part in the national
Gay Pride march
in Huddersfield in
1981, along with the
Gay Icebreakers, a
socialist group who
helped establish the
famous Gay's The Word
bookshop in London.

Photo by
Peter Scott-Presland

We had to get from the ... park, to the ... what would then have been Huddersfield Polytechnic... We had a sort of whole afternoon of doing entertainment and things there... But we had tremendous excitement getting from the park to the thing, because this is where all the National Front people came out of the woodwork. Once the march was actually dispersed, we became more vulnerable, and stuff like that. So there were groups of skinheads just sort of materialised, round the corner as you were going along the streets and stuff. And ... because we had a banner with us on the Consenting Adults [theatre group] one, we were fairly ... well-placed to react, because we simply just [laughs] took the banner down and like a lance, a battering ram, and just charged into these groups of skinheads and got ... out the other side. And we got through it. I mean, I don't think there were actually any casualties, but it was quite exciting and it was... It felt really good to be doing something like Pride... harnessed to a particular cause.

### PETER, Huddersfield

After continued police raids on Huddersfield's Gemini Club, London Pride decided to move the national march to Huddersfield in 1981 in support of the club's owner, John Addy. Peter took part in the march and remembers the presence of the National Front.

**VAL, Leeds**

Val is pictured here at home.

Geoff Brokate Photography

I came out in my early 30s– or recognised that I wasn't the norm in terms of heterosexuality– and I think it was probably politics ... being involved in feminism, that, I think, played a major part in me coming to recognise that I was a lesbian. Not, at that point, I don't think I felt attracted to other women, it was more I felt in sync with other women and politically wanted to spend my time with other women and it was only gradually that I think I wanted to be with other women, in terms of spending my leisure time. With regard to, I suppose, finding other lesbians, I can't, I mean, fortunately, because I was involved in some feminist activity or women's group stuff in Leeds, that I think I did meet other lesbians. But I didn't always know that I was meeting other lesbians, because it wasn't something you'd just announce, "Oh, by the way, I'm a lesbian. By the way..." I might want to mix with women more than men, but I am not necessarily in search of other lesbians per se– it's people, or women– and I probably met a number of lesbians when I decided ... to have a child through self-insemination. I got to know of another woman who was a lesbian who had had a child and then a few of us, after, I think, I'd had my child, there were other lesbians who were either wanting to do self-insemination or in the process of, and we formed a group and met... Then there was something called 'Northern Older Lesbian Network' that doesn't exist anymore but went for about 20-25 years, and that was set up by two lesbians who had moved from London to, I think, Howarth, and that was once a month... And more currently, because there's been like huge gaps in between, it's been being involved in LGBT things like [the group] 'Out In Leeds', like West Yorkshire Queer Stories, like Sage [Leeds' over-50s LGBT+ network] and the current Women's Space.

### PATRICK, Leeds

Patrick was the first openly gay candidate to stand for election in Leeds. In 1988, when this story takes place, his party, Labour, didn't win the seat. 14 years later, he was successfully elected, becoming the city's first openly gay councillor.

Geoff Brokate Photography

One man came up to me – I must have been outside one of the polling stations – and he said, "Oh yes, you're one of the Labour candidates aren't you?" And I said, "Yes, that's right." And he said, "Well, I looked at your leaflet," and he said, "there's just one thing I'm not happy with." And I thought, "Oh God, here we go... I bet I know what it's going to be about..." He said, "You talk about... You say you're gay, and talk about lesbian and gay rights." Anyway, he spoke and said he was not happy with this at all, and went on, and he was polite enough, but made his position clear. I thought, well, we've obviously lost his vote, but hopefully he's just in a minority. And I thought, well, I'd better just ask if he has voted, because, just at least ask him. And I said, "Well, are you going to vote Labour?" fully expecting him to say no. But he said, "What do you mean, am I going to vote Labour? I voted for you at nine o'clock this morning!" And you know, that was absolutely amazing, and I thought, "Oh thank you." And, y'know, I was taken aback, and I said, "Thanks a lot for that," and he went away, almost quite offended that I'd asked him.

**INFO**

**BRADFORD GAY**
**no. 16**    *FREE*

E.M.
FORSTER

GAY
-WRITERS
(FROM THE CLOSET)

*Bradford In The Pink
Programme Inside!*

The 16th issue of *BRADFORD GAY*
newsletter (October, 1985) offered a
wealth of support to its readership
on its back page.

Contributed by Colin Lloyd

It [Bradford Lesbian Line] ran Thursday nights, seven [until] nine, "30-55-25, we await your call". And then we tried it Monday afternoon, because we was getting criticism that, you know, some women couldn't use the phone on an evening, it was difficult. Then we put the answerphone on. Answer phones started coming in in the '80s. So that was good, so we'd then do ring-backs and we used to meet people. Take them to the Bavaria, take them down Oak Lane to the Park Hotel. Crazy stuff. On Tuesday nights. And, I mean, you'd get people coming out relationships, you'd get people with mental health problems... And we used to do film days down at the Playhouse and Film Theatre as fundraisers. And we'd 300 women turn up to see *Desert Hearts* one Saturday afternoon. And we, we had to do two sittings, you know, they were going mad about the insurance. We'd cooked a load of soup in the kitchen and we're selling the soup so [pause]– they were good times, they were good– they, they probably wouldn't happen now. And ... lesbian balls, Victoria Hall. I remember down my socks I had a thousand quid in cash, stuffed down my socks, 'cos we took so much money on the door. Because we didn't pre-sell the tickets in those days, it was cash, I was just literally rolling the cash up and sticking it down my socks.

## LORRAINE, Bradford

Lorraine started going out in Bradford in the late 1970s on what she describes as a friendly lesbian and gay scene. In 1980, she and some friends established a local lesbian helpline with support from the university, in an office on Laisteridge Lane.

**JESSICA, Wakefield**

Jessica is a musician, songwriter and performer, with a third album due in 2020. She's pictured here at home.

Geoff Brokate Photography

Forward to … 17th November 2015, when I had my GRS, my surgery. Actually, no, no– let's go to nine months before that. Nine months before that– that's an appropriate number, isn't it?! Nine months before that, I went to Brighton Gender Clinic … I went to see the surgeon … and he looked at my levels, and he looked and he said, "Y'know…" He looked at everything and said, "No problems, no problems, you're sorted. We'll be able to do this - but I want to get you checked out."

Now, the place where they sent me … had an MRI, and they put me on MRI and said, after various bits of to-ing and fro-ing, "Thought so, you've got an ovary. You've got an ovary and part of a uterus … which is weird, because you've got both your testicles. So, all we can think of really is that it's an absorbed twin. And it's more than likely that your mood swings…" 'Cos, you know, I've kept a journal– sorry a little side note– I've kept a journal since about 1986. It's not frequent, but I keep them all, and y'know, it's… Looking back, I see mood swings happening in various times of the month, and it turns out I was having a period [laughs]! What the hell?! This is a bit weird! Very, very strange!

And um, yeah, so I went and had my GRS [Gender Reassignment Surgery] on the 17th November, 2015. The clock in the room was set to 3:20 and 40 seconds; it had stopped, and so you know, 3:20 and 40 seconds is the time, it's that little bubble, and for five or six days I was in that room, in this little morphine-induced haze and, according to my Mum, when I came out of the theatre and went into recovery, she'd never seen such a big smile, ever. It was like everything was alright, and it's, when I said earlier, it's like background distraction. If you wire up a … if you wire up a sound system wrong, you get a hum. It was like somebody had turned the background hum off. And, yeah, so it turns out that, I mean y'know, yeah, transgender covers it, but actually intersex, and it's, y'know, it's a weird body [laughs].

The LGBT+ choir, Gay Abandon, appear on Ilkey Moor in the 2020 fairytale film *Riding West on a Walrus Tail* created by Jaron Hill and Angelina Jesson and commissioned by West Yorkshire Queer Stories.

Image: Jesson-Hill

So Gay Abandon ... When I first set it up I didn't really have much experience ... of spending time with gay men and suddenly we had a lot of men in the choir ... who I didn't know ... and, well, I didn't know a lot of the women either, so we had a lot of time getting to know each other. Back in those days some of the lesbians in the choir, they also didn't know how to be around gay men. In fact, I remember we had a party at Frances' house and she said, "I haven't had a man in the house for 15 years, since somebody came to mend the roof!"

We were two different groups of people who didn't know how to be in the same room together, but bringing us together through song did also bring us together as friends and, over the years, I think we've become very, very close and it's been a really valuable place for me to form friendships with men, as well as women.

**JANE, Leeds**
Jane founded Gay Abandon in 1997.

**HASAN, Bradford**

Hasan is 17 and recently came out to his mum. He likes to socialise in local queer youth groups and particularly enjoys QTIPOC groups like Late Night Tea, where members of the QTIPOC community take turns hosting a free get-together in their home.

Geoff Brokate Photography

Queer is like a massive part of my identity. But also what is a massive part is my South Asian ... like, my brownness, as well. With the whole intersecting identities, growing up as brown and growing up as queer, I felt like I was sort of battling between the two identities. And I remember just, like, sitting on my bed thinking, "I'm going to have to live a double life. I'm never going to be openly out as a brown person."
And I think that's how it was for quite a while. Especially, because growing up, I didn't believe that brown or black people could even be queer. I thought it was more sort of like a white thing. And it's quite ironic for it to be a white thing, because if you look at colonisation, and then we look at how all these homophobic laws were created by white people, I think that's one of the main reasons why a lot of people of colour have an issue with queerness and transness. And that doesn't just disappear overnight, and it definitely affects the notions that we have of queerness today, as well.

## Five evenings of queer cinema

come for gender-bending cinema that makes you think
queer trash and horror in the campest of settings
features & shorts that take us beyond the queer 'scene'
take in some history & current struggles in the queer world

**Queer:** Defies definition, rejects restrictive gender
and sexuality binaries, all inclusive and non exclusive,
fluid and changeable, anti-heteropartriachy.

Queer Mutiny North is a DIY collective that puts on free
queer events and gatherings in the Leeds area. All film
showings are free, donations are welcome but there will
be no obligation... everyone welcome

At a secret location... text 07966570044 to get
text updates or to arrange sleeping space if you are
coming from out of Leeds.

Money raised will go to Bent Bars, a letter-writing
project for lesbian, gay, bisexual, transgender, transsexu-
al, gender-variant, intersex & queer prisoners in Britain.
www.co-re.org/bentbars

Flyer from the 2nd
Leeds Queer Film
Festival, 22nd to 26th
September, 2010.

There was a squat on Hanover Square, which is like, quite central in town. It's kinda like round the back of the LGI [Leeds General Infirmary], near the university, also known as Hungover Square … Legover Square. There was this big building, which you know was totally intimidating, terrifying, but like really amazing as well 'cos they'd have … it was basically a queer squat, huge, and they had a film festival there. There was a big room and they skipped a load of couches and they built tiered seating out of couches, which blew my mind. And at that film festival, it was like really down-and-dirty, and there was like a dressing-up room and you could do facial hair, there was just like a little teacup full of like bits of hair someone had cut off that you could like … you stuck Vaseline on and stuck it on. So there was a lot of that. It was, everyone just slept in a big heap and like, yeah, it kind of blew my mind really.

**KATHLEEN, Leeds**

Kathleen started coming to Leeds from Sheffield around 2006 to enjoy the city's queer subculture that included gigs, parties and festivals.

## HUSEIN, Leeds

Husein is pictured here at the Stop the Brexit Coup rally organised by Leeds for Europe in Victoria Gardens, Leeds, on 14 September, 2019.

Geoff Brokate Photography

I was born and raised Muslim. My mother, as I mentioned, she's Christian, and my uncle is a retired vicar, so I had some opening and exposure to Christianity from that point of view... To me, it just felt natural... Being gay is natural, like breathing, so I didn't feel inappropriate at all. I didn't feel conflict about being gay and Muslim at all, because I know myself. I mean, I know if I did something wrong, then I'd ask forgiveness for it. Being gay is not a choice: it's something you're born with. And that's how I felt, at the time, and I am the type of person who follows sometimes his gut feeling, rather than thinking, and I just went with it. So I was very comfortable being gay and Muslim.

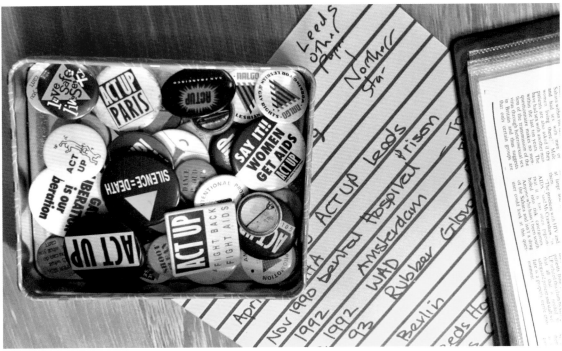

**Gill:** This is a collection of ACT UP badges from, actually, around the world. So, ACT UP – we used the same sort of graphic style that ACT UP New York had developed. I can't remember what they were called... was it Grand Fury? The design collective that did ACT UP visuals. Great graphic images and the logo for ACT UP was this lovely, neat logo that was black on white.

**Mick:** I love 'em! They come from a punk sensibility, which I think is another link, because I think we were all post-punk-ish. And then you've got the classic slogan... You can't say 'ACT UP' without going...?

**Jude:** Fight back, fight AIDS!

**Mick:** We had a lot of call and responses, didn't we? There was: ACT UUUUUP!

**Jude:** FIGHT BACK, FIGHT AIDS!

**Mick:** People with AIDS, under attack, what do we do?

**Jude and Gill:** ACT UP! FIGHT BACK!

**Mick:** If you're of that age you remember those stiff badges: 'Fuck safe, ACT UP', 'Dance Proud, ACT UP', 'Shoot Clean, ACT UP' and we had T-shirts with 'Fuck Safe, Dance Proud, Shoot Clean', which was quite a wild one to wear at work occasionally!

**Jude:** I remember we got 'ACT UP Leeds' put on a T-shirt. And, again, we were poor – we didn't have any money for the T-shirts – so we managed to find a T-shirt company who would print them really, really cheaply. And when they arrived they were all absolutely massive, weren't they?! And that's my memory of so many demonstrations– all these T-shirts down to our knees!

**Gill:** I think they fell apart!

IMAGE TOP: **ACT UP Leeds (AIDS Coalition To Unleash Power) came together in 1990 to raise awareness of AIDS and demand funding for research and treatment. This photograph was taken in 1991, and is from the ACT UP Leeds collection. Gill appears far left.**

IMAGE BOTTOM: **ACT UP badge collection**

**ROBERT, Leeds**

A regular at the Gemini nightclub in Huddersfield during its
heyday in the late 1970s and early 80s. He's pictured on the
spot where a door once led to the famous former venue.

Geoff Brokate Photography

What the Gemini did on Sundays … they used to run a free bus from Lower Briggate [in Leeds] on Sunday nights. I think it was about eight o'clock. They used to take you to the Gemini and it only stayed open until midnight on Sundays, but they gave you a supper, 'cos they had to do that in order to get the licence. One night, we were disco-ing and everything was going really, really well, and then there was this noise: "Everybody stop!" The lights came on and about 10 or 15 coppers appeared, say[ing], "Right, nobody's leaving here 'til we get your names and addresses!" This policewoman came over to me – she says, "Right, can I have your name?" So I said, "No." I thought to myself, "Well, I've done nothing wrong. Why should I give my name and address?" And we were just stood there, and I thought, "Oh God the bus has probably gone. We're gonna be stranded here." And, erm, the police then just turned round and went down the steps. And, as they were going down the steps, they must have found this record from round the back somewhere, but they played 'God Save Our Gracious Queen' and we all started laughing.

The Gemini, on Huddersfield's Southgate, was widely considered the best gay nightclub in the north of England in the late 1970s and early 80s.

Photographs by John Addy,
who managed the Gemini
for five years from October,
1976 to October, 1981.

**IAN, Leeds**

Ian moved from South Shields
to West Yorkshire to attend
Huddersfield Polytechnic in 1981.
He's called it home ever since.

Geoff Brokate Photography

I'd actually heard of the Gemini from people in Newcastle, because it was famous– or infamous– throughout the country. People did come from all over the country to go to the Gemini... I remember there were some of the classic stereotypes there. There was a leather man with a huge moustache, a walrus moustache. In fact, a lot of people had big moustaches then (it was very much the fashion in the early eighties). 'Clones', they were called. The classic clone look was close-cropped hair, big moustache, checked shirt, jeans, black shoes and often white socks. I was more of a New Romantic at that time. I had an extremely long blonde fringe, just sort of covering one eye, and I think my fringe came down to my chin, and then the side bit was cropped really close. It was an adaptation of Phil Oakey from the Human League's look, except with blonde hair, rather than black hair ... and lots of sort of floaty clothes.

**Charlie's Nightclub**

Many a night out in 1970s Leeds ended up at Charlie's. With landlords Noel and Joe, Charlie's provided an entertaining place for the LGBT+ community to meet once the pubs closed.

Lower Briggate continues as the city's main destination for the LGBT+ community and its allies.

#RainbowPlaques

Supported by @StudioTDH

Rainbow Heritage Plaque at the entrance to Queen's Court, Leeds, formely Charlie's Nightclub.

Image courtesy of Leeds Civic Trust

**Like a record, baby**

Last night, a boy told me
he'd travelled over 4,000 miles
to dance at Queens Court
and that if he spun fast enough
really fast
he could make the world rotate
a little quicker,
days glimmer that bit sooner
back home
for people like him.
For people like me.
*Come, hold my hand, he said,*
*and don't let go*
*or we'll fall off the edge.*
He vanished before the slow songs.

Ian Humphreys

The bar and nightclub named in this poem is
Queens Court, a fixture of the Leeds gay scene
since 1996, which is mentioned in several WYQS
interviews. (The gay venue, Charlie's Nightclub,
had occupied its spot on Lower Briggate in
previous decades.)

Ian Humphrey's intention in the piece was "to
link, through surreal imagery, queer people living
in relatively free and safe Western cities to those
who are unable to 'be themselves' in their home
country, because going to a gay club, for example,
would be too risky."

To Connie with love. Jason

Fartown Fruits
Jacuzzi Paradise

All profits from this record go to
ACT-UP AIDS Coalition To Unleash Power

Don't Fall in and Out of Love

Special thanks to Brendan Croker, Johnny Langford, Baby Fabb, Guy and Phil at Lion Studios, Leeds

SNAT 117

5 020958 011779

Fartown Fruits were an alternative queer band active in the Leeds-Bradford area in the late 1980s and early 90s, and named after a grocer's shop in Huddersfield.

I have a chronic illness that affects me physically, so I walk with a stick, basically, 99.9% of the time, and I have chronic pain. So I think, for me, one of the things I notice is, when I tell people you have chronic pain, their instant reaction is that you can't be, you mustn't be able to be sexual at all. Now... [Laughs.] This kind of becomes a problem when you're in an LGBT space– if you're in a gay bar, anywhere like that– that people just don't, just sense that you're, just don't speak to you, 'cos clearly you're not capable of doing those things and clearly... But then it's like, once people get the double-whammy of: "Oh, did you know I'm also gay and identify as bisexual?" And they're like: "Whaaat?!" [Laughs.] It kind of like blows their mind. Like, I find that really difficult ... difficult to meet somebody because of that. They make instant assumptions by the fact you've got a stick, that you just can't physically engage in those things, when you definitely can.

**BECCA, Leeds**

Becca is originally from Lancashire but lives and studies in Leeds.

**JOHN, Leeds**

John lives in Wakefield, but
worked in Leeds for many years.

Geoff Brokate Photography

1981... I used to come home from Leeds up Swinegate to the station and on the corner of a little yard I now know as Blayds Yard, there was a bookshop that sold 'dirty'– in inverted commas– magazines. One day, one of these magazines caught my eye and for some reason I bought it. And in it, I learnt about AIDS for the first time. It wasn't called AIDS then– 'gay plague' I think they called it– it later became H3, then H4, and then HIV. This article mentioned this disease that was affecting the gay population in California and America and it described it [as] a nasty disease and people were dying from it, but it wasn't widespread; it was just confined to a certain area and– as they put it– it was "as rare as rocking horse shit", so there was nothing really to worry about.

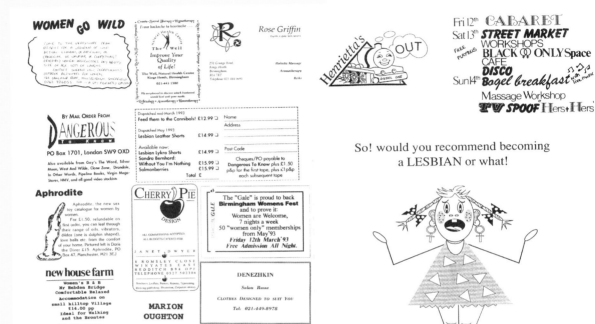

From the programme for Henrietta's OUT Lesbian Fun Weekend, 12th to 14th March, 1993.

Without lesbians, or without lesbian feminists,
Women's Aid wouldn't ever have existed,
nor would Rape Crisis, nor would the other
campaigns about violence against women,
like the Zero Tolerance campaign; nor would
Reclaim The Night. Lesbian feminists were the
backbone of all of those campaigns. It could
have been because fewer lesbian feminists had
children. I mean, childcare was always an issue.
But then, lesbian feminists were also lesbian
mothers and had very strong campaigns for
lesbian mothers, and to try and get the feminist
movement to support lesbian mothers, and to
help lesbian mothers get pregnant with cans of
sperm being carried across the city in thermos
flasks. You wouldn't believe! [Laughs.] And it
worked. There was a bit of a concern, because
a lot of the children who emerged from that
were boys, and we thought "Hmm, what is this?"
but there was, you know, a sprinkling of girls as
well [chuckles]. And they all turned out to be
completely wonderful and delightful children.

## LAL, Leeds

Lal has lived in Leeds since 1964. In
the early 1970s, she was involved in
setting up a women's liberation group
in the city.

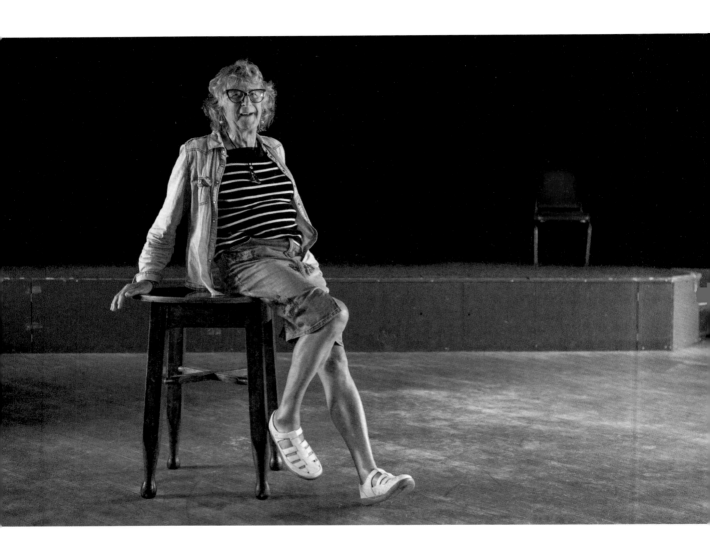

**HELEN, Keighley**

Helen is pictured here at the Trades Club in Hebden Bridge. She's been with her partner for 25 years.

Geoff Brokate Photography

When I got my, um, Gender Recognition Certificate, we re-did our marriage, from being male-female to being female-female… You could only do this … I can't remember the date, but there was a date when it happened, that same-sex [couples] could marry, rather than [have] a civil partnership. And, when we applied to re-register our marriage as female-female they asked us, "Now, do you want it on the date that the law changed, or do you want to retain your original date?" And we said we wanted to retain our original date. And what they said in the registry office, they said, "Basically, if you don't put the date of the new law, people will know." And we thought, "Well, does it really matter? We were married on this day and this is our anniversary and this is the day, not the day the law changed." So … we're still together and she's still supporting me and I'm still supporting her… I'm one of the real fortunates amongst the trans community, that many, many trans people lose their relationships, but I didn't and, um, it's been the most wonderful thing. I think it's the most wonderful thing. And it's not been without trauma for my partner. It's not been without trauma– she's had a lot of trauma– but we've reached a stage, I think, where we just get on with life. We don't worry too much about anything.

# INTRODUCTION.

Hi!, Welcome to "IN YER FACE". A magazine for young lesbian women in the Bradford area.

It's the happening magazine that you need to find out what's new and what lies ahead in the future of life today.

Aren't you sick and tired of hearing about coming events taking place in London or some far away town that takes hours to get there and is costly. Well, this is the magazine to brings things closer to home.

"IN YER FACE", is designed to directly put things in your face. The up-to-date account of what's going on in the area, so you won't be in the dark about the most important events in the calender.

"IN YER FACE", will cover news articles keeping you up-to-date with the latest goings on in the lesbian, gay and straight worlds. There will be reviews of events, books, music and anything else we care to mention. The fashion page will keep you in style with the latest dyke wear. Advertisements throughout the magazine will inform you of the nearest lesbian friendly pubs and businesses. The problem page aims to iron out any of those unwanted hassles in your life. Or maybe you'll find out your destiny by reading your stars. We'll keep you up-to-date on trips out, events and residentials happening within the group and outside the group. So why not join us and come along. The magazine will also include interviews, special features, personal stories, classifies and surveys.

We will always keep you up-to-date with news of the lesbian drop-in, to let you know how things are progressing, so hopefully it will lead to you dropping in to see us.

So I hope you will enjoy reading this first edition of "IN YER FACE". Remember this is your magazine, so if you have any idea's or articles to print don't hesitate to contact us, we will be willing to publish any worthy material.

Enjoy the read and keep up-to-date with "IN YER FACE".
    Best regards,
    Carla and the 'In Yer Face' Crew

The first issue of *IN YER FACE*, aimed at young lesbians in Bradford, came out in 1994.

Contributed by Norrina Rashid

I've got some magazines which we created... The magazine was called *IN YER FACE*, and what it was was that young people– and you've gotta remember– I feel a bit embarrassed at people looking at these, that this is pre-social media days. Young people couldn't connect with each other, do y'know? There was no easy way of making contact. So a group of young people decided to put this magazine together and it was literally written on a typewriter, it was literally cut out with a pair of scissors, and it was literally stuck down with glue and then it was photocopied and then heat-bound. And we sent these magazines out locally. We got a list of queer youth groups within the Yorkshire area, within the North, let's say, but then we got ... we realised there was a demand for the magazine. But anyway, we had articles in it, y'know, book reviews, stuff about youth groups, activities that we do. We had the stars, the horoscopes... I think we were quite creative about that! We had groups of young people none of this was done by adults. I was the only worker who was literally making sure that it was printed, but the whole contents and stuff was led and run by young people and obviously I had to kind of overlook it, to make sure that everything that went in it was okay from the point of view of, y'know, safeguarding, let's say. So, yeah, they set up a penpal scheme, and people from other countries would subscribe to it.

## NORRINA, Bradford

Norrina grew up in Bradford, where she became a youth worker in the early 1990s. She helped establish the city's first LGBT youth group and also set up the UK's first residential for young black queers.

## ALI, Leeds

Ali is the chair of Leeds Pride and is pictured here on the main stage of the 2019 event on Lower Briggate.

Geoff Brokate Photography

The first Leeds Pride ... there [were] 300 people. We were stood on the stairs outside the Civic Hall: there was no staging, no nothing. We had 300 people going down the Headrow waving rainbow flags. There was no one lining the streets to watch. There was a police van at the front, a police van at the back, and that was pretty much the parade. We got to Lower Briggate and were like, "What do we do now?".

Last year it was about 6,000 participants in the parade and tens of thousands lining the streets. The streets were lined all the way from Millennium Square, all the way down to Kirkgate Market and beyond, two or three deep. It was fantastic to see how the event has grown over the last 14 or so years.

**FLO, Bradford**

Flo grew up in Keighley. They became an active member of the Campaign for Nuclear Disarmament in Bradford as a teenager, meeting friends at the community-run Treehouse Cafe and nearby housing co-operative, Branches.

Geoff Brokate Photography

I came to my queerness in a very politicised way. It was through meeting those people in Bradford and learning about housing co-ops, which is, for me, an explicitly political way of organising housing. And, through those things, I started to meet trans people and queer people, and for a while I was like, "Oh, how interesting; how intellectually interesting," which I hear is common among us folk. And then, as I made more friends and began to feel comfortable that there were people like me ... I started to kind of open up in that way, and that very slowly got the wheels turning, like: "Oh, oh, I think I'm ... I mean, I'm definitely not straight ... Oh, I'm also trans. Riiiight, OK!"

I often wonder how much later it would have been if my life had gone differently in my teenage years, 'cos I think, coming at it from such a politicised point of view, there was already less shame ... I was already in an environment where, as far as other people were concerned anyway, it was fine. And I think that would have been harder if I weren't in those kind of environments.

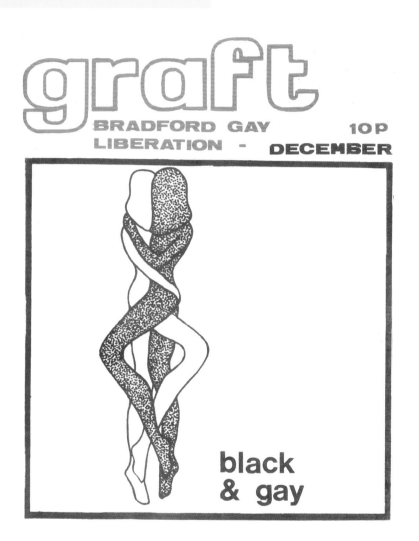

# graft

**BRADFORD GAY LIBERATION -** 10P **DECEMBER**

**black & gay**

*GRAFT*, the newsletter of
Bradford Gay Liberation
Front, from December, 1976.

Contributed by Colin Lloyd

You know the TV series Empire? Empire actually really helped me to have a conversation with my Mum about my sexuality, because on Empire there's a gay son, and the gay son's father's mistreating him, because he's gay. He really gives him a hard time. And my mum, we were watching it, and she was just like, "I don't understand why he's giving them such a hard time … just 'cause he's gay doesn't matter." And I was in shock! I was sat across with my Mum and my jaw was on the floor. I was like, are you actually kidding? It made me rage! 'Cause it was like, "This is like strangers. It's not even like real people and they're on a TV show! And you can connect with that, but you can't connect with me and I'm your daughter. Like what is going on here?"

It did turn into a massive argument and then we calmed down and we had a chat and … part of the argument was, well, "He was always obviously gay to his dad, because it showed flashbacks from when he's a kid", she says. "You didn't show any signs of this. I didn't know. It just all happened all of a sudden!" I was like, "Whoa! OK. So that's where this came from."

Now I can understand a bit. She'd just been thrown into a war zone. And it kind of just made more sense… I could see it in her eyes that she'd got it. She's just all of a sudden got it… That she needed to either understand that this was happening and … maybe she's not happy about it, but she needs to change her behaviour and language towards me, so that we could still be mother and daughter, and be able to have a relationship of some kind together. And she just said to me, "You know, this is really difficult for me and I'm trying." She said, "I'm trying"… And that's all I needed for her to say.

### VANESSA, Bradford

Vanessa moved to the north of England from Birmingham at the age of 10 and currently lives in Bradford. She's moved around the UK, but says that she inevitably returns to Yorkshire "like a homing pigeon".

Clive's story happened in 1974 and is illustrated by project volunteer, Gill, who carried out the original interview.

When I told my Mum I was, that I was gay, she said, would I go to see the doctor, the GP? So I said, "OK". So I went, and he looked a bit sort of uncomfortable, and he said, "Well, what do you want me to do?" I said, "I've no idea." He said, "Well, I think I should arrange for you to see a psychiatrist." I said, "OK." So I went to see this psychiatrist, and this psychiatrist said, "Well, what do you want me to do?" And I said, "Well, I don't know." And he said, "Well, you can have therapy if you like." And I'd seen– I think I must have been about 18 or 19– I'd seen on World in Action on telly, a programme about aversion therapy involving electric shocks and sexy pictures and so on. And I said, "Do you mean that?" And he said, "Yes." And I said, "No way!" And he said, "Well, do you want to see a psychologist?" And I said, "Well, what does that involve?" And he said, "Talking." So I said, "OK, I'll do that."

So, I went to see this psychologist over a period of maybe a few months or something. And eventually this psychologist said, "I want you to buy some [straight] pornography." [Laughs.] So, I said, "OK." And he said, "Let me know what effect it has on you." So, I didn't know where to buy pornography apart from WH Smiths. I think I'd seen Playboy or something like that. So I went to WH Smiths and I got this pornography. And so I went back and he said, "What effect did it have on you?" And I said, "Well, not much." So he said, "Well, I think you're gay. I think you should go away and be happy!" [Laughs.] So, that was the end of that and I told my Mum and she wasn't impressed!

**CLIVE, Wakefield**
Clive grew up in Wakefield and attended Leeds College of Music, where he fought for the rights of LGB students in the 1980s.

### YVETTE & KAREN, Leeds

Yvette remembers going to women's discos in Leeds in the early 1990s around Roundhay, Chapel Allerton, and on the university campus. She still lives in Leeds with her partner Karen, whom she's been with since 2004. They're pictured here together at home in their garden.

Geoff Brokate Photography

**Yvette:** Oh yeah, the women's discos, well there was a thing that we wanted women-only discos, because it wasn't around, y'know? Women wanted a place to feel safe, to feel relaxed and stuff ... It was a lot of Gabrielle! Gabrielle was played. Y'know, that kind of music that were in the charts in the early 90s. Y'know, there was like dance music ... and female artists like, um, Alison Moyet and Gabrielle ... Belinda Carlisle, yes! [Laughs.] And of course, we used to let our hair down, because it was all women and, at the end of the night, because there was so many drunken people, they went topless. [Laughs.] That was the excitement of the evening! All these women just taking their bras off and their t-shirts and just dancing, y'know, and it's like, it's like, "Okay!" [Laughs.]

But it was a space for us to feel secure and [we] knew that we wasn't threatened or anything, yeah. We didn't have a fear that something was going to happen. We did have a couple of bouncers on the doors to keep people out that shouldn't be there, y'know, but no, it was great, y'know. The live acts used to be absolutely brilliant. You used to be able to enjoy yourself and let your hair down. I don't think they do it as much now, with promotions and stuff, but yeah, it was absolutely fantastic.

**PAULINE, Leeds**

Pauline, pictured here at home, is a
member of the local LGBT+ Women's
Space.

Geoff Brokate Photography

I am a trans woman, mature in age, if not in wisdom [others chuckling] and I have been in Leeds 26 years and it has been, you know, a great blessing to me in many ways... It's been very important to me, as has this group where I have found a kind of welcome and acceptance and been included, which has made a big difference to my life, which changed hugely, you know, when I transitioned, which was only five years ago, so I don't have a long experience of being in the LGBT community, but the experience I have had since then has been an extremely positive one, which I am grateful for.

I have recently become quite close to a trans-masculine person, i.e. somebody genetically female but who has transitioned to becoming a man and it's been a fascinating encounter getting to know that person. This is somebody who is almost ... many, sort of, might think of as the ideal man actually, because it's a man who has had the experience of also trying to live as a woman and in transitioning and becoming a man, he's trying to not fall... Not, not be the kind of man that, when he was living as a woman, he would have disliked and been oppressed by.

So, I have learnt a great deal from talking to him and I would recommend that if anybody has the chance to get to know a trans-masculine person, because a lot of the discourse about trans people tends to be about trans women and there are a lot of trans men around as well and they have a fascinating experience to share with us and to learn from, I think.

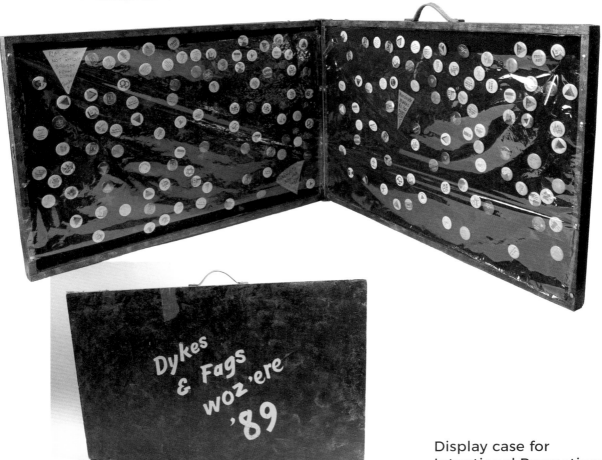

Display case for Intentional Promotions' badge collection.

The idea really started [for the Intentional Promotions campaign]... as we first found out about Clause 28, and everybody, like we just felt really shitty, it was a really shitty time to be around and we were really isolated and lonely. And a few of us that had found each other were finally starting to feel okay, and then the law was proposed and it just felt like the biggest blow in the world. And I remember standing up at the Gay Society, 'cos we were discussing we should do something and we didn't know what to do. And I stood up, and I remember saying, 'I want to intentionally promote homosexuality'. I shocked myself. I shocked everybody else. I remember doing that, because it was like, 'We can't do that, that's just wrong.' But I just thought if they're accusing us of that anyway then we might as well just do it. And then the plan was to try and work out how to do it, which we didn't know.

And then we went into the Christmas break while we all thought about it and we came back in the January and we decided we needed to do something. So we all piled down to London really early on a march and things and saw people and it was amazing and we got to see some of the old GLF badges, the Gay Liberation Front stuff, and thought, 'We wanna do something.' And we knew there was a badge machine at the university, so we decided to start making big badges and we sat round and collected slogans... the bestseller was, 'I'm straight, but it might just be a phase.

## JACKIE, Leeds

Jackie founded the campaigining collective, 'Intentional Promotions' in 1988, with her friend, Rob Preston, in Leeds. Together, they toured university campuses distributing badges with pro-lesbian and gay slogans.

### CHAR, Loughborough

Char's parents came from Yorkshire and, after a
Scottish upbringing, she relocated for many years
to Huddersfield, followed by Hebden Bridge. She
is pictured here in her garden at home.

Geoff Brokate Photography

My mum caught us in bed together [starts laughing] when I was 14. So Rachel was 'the older woman' (she was 15). And my mum immediately rang the police, and then was absolutely furious to find out that it wasn't a crime! So then she marched me off to the doctor to get some pills to 'sort me out' and– thank God– turned out my doctor was a lesbian. I mean, how likely was that?

**Trans Pride Leeds, 2018**

Photograph by Jamie Fletcher

It felt amazingly powerful, it was pouring with rain, it was freezing, it was 31st March, Trans Day of Visibility, and we were certainly very fricking visible. It felt so unexpectedly powerful, because I'd been in Pride marches before ... but it was a smaller number of us taking up a bigger space and I was at the front and what was most interesting was the reactions, really, by the passers-by... When you do the general LGBT Pride ... everybody knows that Pride is happening, everything is covered in rainbows, there are rows and rows of people lined up to watch the parade ... everyone is supportive and knows why you're there.

Trans Pride, no one was prepared, and people were turning round, just staring in incomprehension and slight fear, really, at what we were doing. It wasn't hostility, but it was kind of bafflement... There wasn't a layer of 'everyone round me is supporting me'. It felt genuinely revolutionary, I guess, genuinely disruptive to people's lives, which I guess, you know, is what Pride used to feel like...

### KIT, Leeds

Kit reflects on Trans Pride Leeds in 2018, the first trans, non-binary and intersex Pride march in the North of England.

**JORDAN, Leeds**

Pictured at the Carriageworks in Leeds, Jordan was 'born and bred' in the city. He established the inclusive club night, Be LGBTQ: R'n'B with Edges, here in 2016.

Geoff Brokate Photography

[The club night] Be LGBTQ was born in 2016 and it came about because I'd been going out on the gay scene, and then on the straight scene as well with friends, for about 10 years. I've got a real passion for R'n'B music, and I'd find that I'd either have to go to straight places like Norman's, or Fruit Cupboard, which is now Backroom, or Revolution, or wherever to hear R'n'B music, but not be able to flirt with guys. Whereas, when I went out with my gay friends, it was to go to Queens Court, Fibre, Mission, flirt with guys, but then, be a bit depressed about the music policy!

So I just decided, let's think of this brand, it's called 'Be LGBTQ' and its offshoot from that is 'R'n'B with Edges' ... and describe what we wanna play: R'n'B with music at the focus, and then we want the edges to be rap, dancehall, house, and still have pop there, y'know from more traditional LGBTQ venues, but just make it so much more funky and soulful and passionate. I wanted a night that incorporated all that, and it wasn't really about it being a Black night, even though it's music of Black origin and I'm a black man, a proud, black, gay man... It was purely about getting people, all nationalities, all cultures, in a room to hear some good music, that were LGBTQ and weren't afraid about being able to express their desires or flirtations for people, but still hear great music as well.

## LUNA, Leeds

Luna describes herself as "an emerging, working-class trans femme gobshite from Leeds". She is also part of the Queerology artist collective and co-coordinator of Non-Binary Leeds. She's pictured here in Wharf Chambers bar and arts venue.

Geoff Brokate Photography

Leeds has gained, over the past few years, a much stronger queer performance scene... I performed at Live Art Bistro as part of a cabaret night, but also did a workshop on the middle floor of Wharf Chambers, where I did a gender reveal party! Which was really, really great. And that was particularly fantastic, because that was the first time I'd ever been paid as a trans person doing trans things. As an artist, it was very exciting, very emotional and just brilliant.

# MESMAG

the newsletter of the Yorkshire MESMAC membership scheme. spring 2000

## Hello and welcome to MESMAG, the first issue of Yorkshire MESMAC's gazette.

As we approach our 10th anniversary it is appropriate that we launch MESMAG. As an organisation we have always been keen that we are open and that local men can have input into shaping local services. Therefore one of the aims of MESMAG is to ensure that local people are aware of the activities of Yorkshire MESMAC, and to act as a forum for debate and consultation.

We are eager to hear your views on any matters that concern the health and wellbeing of Gay men and men who have sex with men. These can range from anything from policing to housing to combination therapies.

This issue of MESMAG will introduce you to some of the work and activities presently being undertaken by Yorkshire MESMAC. Future issues of MESMAG will include: highlights from latest research findings, news on up-coming events, group and community profiles and training opportunities, together with reviews of latest resources.

As an agency we aim to ensure that all homosexually active men have the knowledge, skills, services and resources to make informed choices about the type of sex we have and our wider health. Clearly, no single agency can hope to achieve this aim alone, there is also a recognition that many barriers exist that prevent men from making real choices. Therefore, Yorkshire MESMAC is committed to working in partnership with other agencies to improve access to services and remove barriers to choice.

*continued on page 3*

**The community space in Yorkshire MESMAC's new Leeds city centre premises.
The room is available free to gay groups. Please contact the Leeds office for details of how to use this space. Unfortunately, it is not wheelchair-accessible.**

The first edition of Yorkshire MESMAC's newsletter *MESMAG* published in Spring, 2000 and is introduced by Tom Doyle.

... And then I saw a job for– at Leeds AIDS Advice– which was a voluntary sector response to HIV in Leeds, and that was for a Services Co-ordinator, I think... Something like that. And I applied for that, and I got an interview, and didn't get it. Outrageous! But ... two months later, I got a phone call from the then-manager of Leeds AIDS Advice [who] said, "There's this new project which we've got funded called MESMAC, and it's about– for– gay men, would you apply for that 'cos we really like you." So I did, and I became the first outreach worker for, for Leeds AIDS Advice. Well, we were still on the MESMAC project.

So MESMAC stands for 'Men who have Sex with Men; Action in the Community'. It doesn't fit the acronym at all... It was the first project of its kind to get statutory funded for working with gay and bisexual men around HIV and it was funded by the Health Education Authority.

We did a lot of outreach work in bars and clubs, and that was interesting 'cos at the time we used to get a lot of knock-back and a lot of ... you know, people thinking it was a bit too much in-your-face and we shouldn't be talking about HIV on the scene; and, you know, there was a group of just radical gays sort of banging on about HIV and AIDS when the people wanted to have a drink and that, so you know, there was quite a bit of that actually.

**TOM, Leeds**

Tom is still CEO of Yorkshire Mesmac, now one of the oldest and largest sexual health organisations in the country.

### TRISTAN, Huddersfield

Tristan is an activist and campaigner based in Huddersfield and is pictured on the town's university campus.

Geoff Brokate Photography

There isn't really a lot in Huddersfield... There's the LGBTQ society, that's at the university, and I believe there's the Huddersfield Gay Group as well... I lived in York beforehand and I was involved briefly with a youth group as part of Yorkshire MESMAC... That one was really just a social space for young people, many of whom weren't out to their parents at that point, so it was really nice to have that and to have the chance to meet other trans people, because at that point, I was just coming out and I was the only trans person that I knew, like, I didn't know anyone else. So having that sense of community, I suppose, was nice and that was really helpful. Right now, the way that it's changed my life is so surreal, still, to me.

Just last week I actually won an award as Trans Activist of the Year from NUS [National Union of Students], which is huge. I'm being interviewed by not just the university press, but I got interviewed by the Yorkshire Post, I think, yes, the Yorkshire Post, about the work that I do. I'm meeting with serious committees and things, like I was meeting with the university teaching and learning committee a couple of weeks ago to deliver a paper on trans student experience and people are taking me very seriously as a professional and it's very strange sometimes.

**ROB, Leeds**

Rob established the community initiative Angels
of Freedom in December, 2017, and Leeds
Freedom Families in February, 2019.

Geoff Brokate Photography

The Angels of Freedom ... we look at LGBT community safety and support. We do Friday evening patrols around the Freedom Quarter area, Call Lane, around Wharf Chambers, so concentrating on that area. On our Fridays, we do more of the early intervention, the prevention stuff ... and a lot of it is just about having a little conversation with people and being a friendly face. We get a lot of people who talk to us about mental health and I think for us it's really important that, for some people who are isolated, who are lonely, who are going out on the scene by themselves and not really connecting with people ... for them to stop and have a five or ten minute chat with us. That could be the only real conversation they have with anyone all night, other than ordering drinks at the bar or saying hello to one of the door staff. It means a lot to some people. I know it means a lot to us to be able to provide that.

[The badge] said: 'How dare you presume I'm a heterosexual?' and I started wearing that at work... It was quite a large supermarket which is no longer around in this country ... Sometimes we went out for a leaving do, and I wore my badge, and a girl who I worked with there said, "I know what a homosexual is, but what is a heterosexual?"

### RAYMOND, Leeds

Raymond went to his first committee meeing of the Leeds CHE [Campaign for Homosexual Equality] in 1979 and remains an active member of its offshoot, Leeds Gay Community, today.

# "I know what a homosexual is, but what is a heterosexual?"